THE HOME FRONT
STIRLING
1939–1945

THE HOME FRONT STIRLING 1939–1945

by JAYNE STEPHENSON

STIRLING DISTRICT LIBRARIES

© Jayne Stephenson

Published by
Stirling District Libraries 1991

ISBN 1-8705421-9-3

Printed by
Cordfall Ltd
041 332 4640

Acknowledgements

The author wishes to thank the Smith Art Gallery & Museum, Stirling and George Dixon of Central Regional Archives for the loan of illustrative material. Many thanks are also due to the many people whose memories of the war in Stirling provide the basis for this book. All contributors wished to remain anonymous but without their memories we would know so little about what it was like to live through the war.

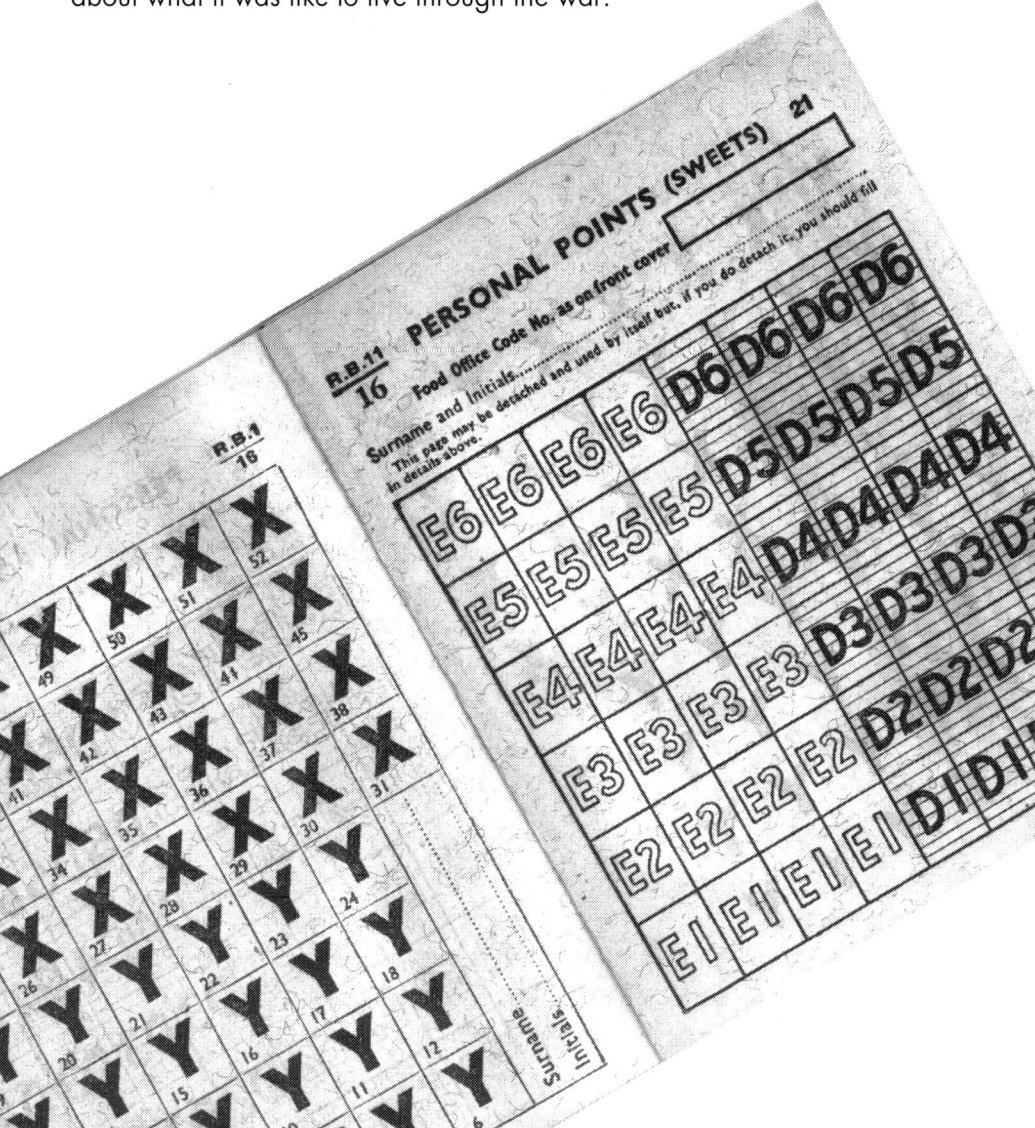

"MY FIRST AIR RAID"
"Journal" Reporter's Vivid Impressions Moonlight Attack on South-East Town
FOOTBALL GRAND STAND DEMOLISHED: FAMILIES RENDERED HOMELESS

FIRST-HAND impressions of a moonlight attack on a Scottish town by a Nazi raider last week-end are given in a "story" which a "Journal" reporter sends us from a town in the south-east of Scotland (where he has been spending a few days). The results — damage to a football grand stand, houses, etc., and a few minor casualties, mostly cuts from flying glass — scarcely seem worth the enemy's expenditure on petrol which the journey cost him.

Two large bombs were dropped by enemy raiders which appeared over a town in south-east Scotland in the early hours of Saturday morning. One of the bombs fell in an open field and another in the grounds of a popular Second Division football club, missing the actual playing pitch by twenty or thirty yards, and in addition to the complete shattering of one wing of the grand stand, a crater 18 feet deep and 40 feet in diameter was caused. Part of the terracing was demolished as well as the press-room, dressing-rooms, and offices. A portion of the entrance and turnstiles was also damaged.

MIRACULOUS ESCAPES.

Many house windows in neighbouring streets were broken, and plate glass in shops in the centre of the town were smashed.

Many people found their doors forced open by the blast, while in other instances difficulty was experienced in getting exit from the houses the following day, the locks having become jammed.

At this stage the raider appears to have been flying low, and one railwayman states that when he heard the roar of the plane as it approached his stationary engine he and his companion jumped out and sheltered beneath the tender. He also stated that he heard the patter of machine gun bullets, and certainly stray bullets have since been picked up in various parts of the town, one piercing a church window and becoming embedded in a pillar in the chancel.

The Home Front

On the 20th July 1940 two bombs were dropped on Stirling, one fell on waste ground causing no damage, but the other hit the King's Park football ground wrecking the stands, causing an 18 feet deep crater and demolishing part of the terracing. The force of the blast was felt in neighbouring streets, a nearby cottage was almost completely destroyed and shops in the town had their plate glass windows smashed;

We were bombed out in Springfield Place, two o'clock in the morning. The roof wasn't in, but there was a beam through the ceiling. Soot came down and oh, we were in some mess . . .'

AIR-RAID
SOUTH-EAST TOWN BOMBED
HOUSES DAMAGED: FAMILIES HOMELESS

Two large bombs were dropped by a Nazi raider early on Saturday morning on the outskirts of a town in South-East Scotland. One of the bombs fell on a football ground enclosure, and the blast wrecked a row of two-storeyed cottage, and so exstensively damaged a row of two-storeyed houses opposite the ground entrance that many families were rendered homeless. There were a number of casualties, all of which were stated to be slight.

The other bomb fell farther into the country.

In the cottage near the football ground a Mr and Mrs Hugh McColl were in an upstairs bedroom, and their two daughters, Miss Minnie and Miss Anne, were in a bedroom on the ground floor. Mr McColl's injuries necessitated his removal to an infirmary. His daughters received slight cuts. Residing in another part of the same building were Mrs Tom Tetstall and her young son required institutional treatment, after being extricated from the debris. Mrs Tetstall and her children were saved from serious injury because the bed they were in half-telescoped and gave them a ready-made safety barrier from falling masonry. Mr James Campbell was trapped in an upstairs room. A.R.P. men rescued him with a ladder.

The stand and turnstile entrance to the football ground were demolished; windows of houses in the vicinity suffered, and plate-glass windows in the business centre of the town more than a quarter of a mile away were broken.

Some curious incidents are said to have occurred. A goldfish in a bowl in the wrecked cottage had its tail blown off. It seemed to be dead, but when a few drops of brandy were put in the water the goldfish revived. One joiner found the windows of his premises intact, but the locks on his door burst. The handle of a door was forced off and embedded itself in the wall opposite, yet no damage was done to the glass panels.

A.R.P. workers and ambulances were quickly in action, and casualties were speedily removed to an infirmary for treatment.

Families rendered homeless, and who were unable to find refuge with friends, were temporarily lodged in a poor law institution. Accommodation has now been found for them in newly-completed houses built by the local authority.

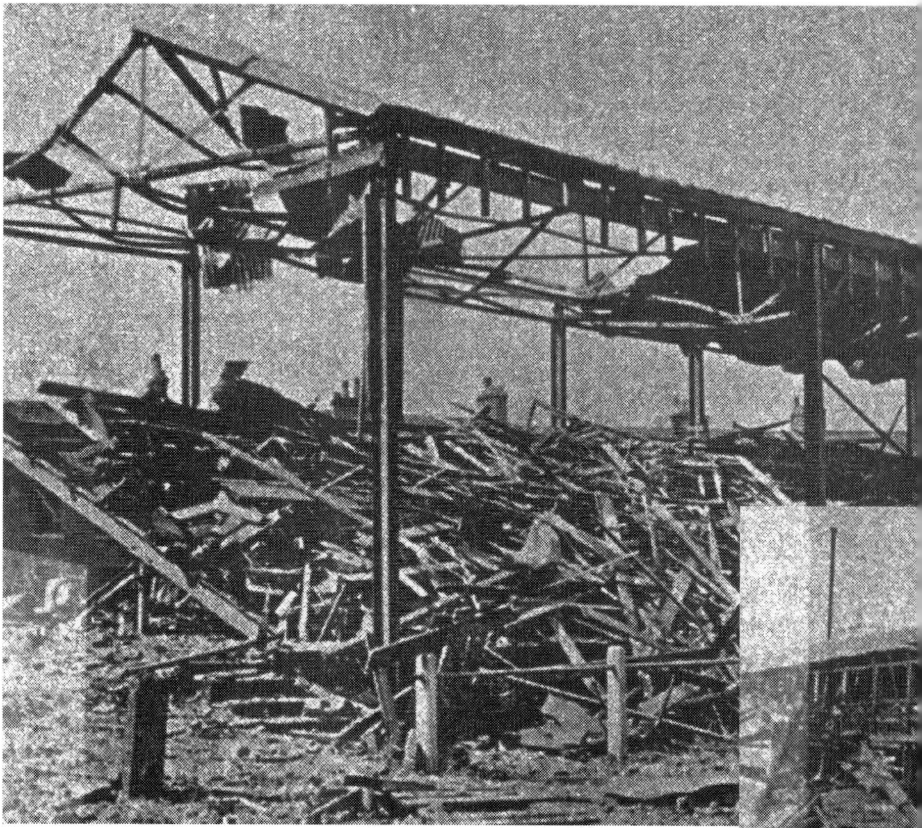

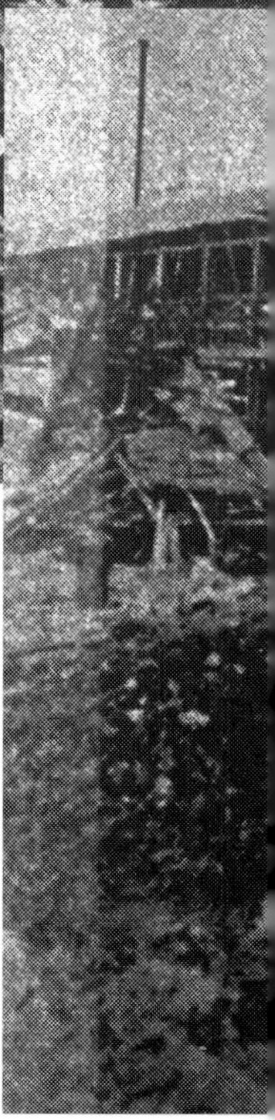

Why do German Bombers pick on our Football Grounds?

This was Stirling's only experience of the war first hand but the people of Stirling fought their own war from the very beginning, losing loved ones fighting on the Front, coping with rationing, changing jobs and taking in evacuees. It was a time of great disruption and change to family life and people coped by fighting and winning their own war on the *Home Front*.

A CHEERFUL STORY

PUBLIC MORALE AT ITS HEIGHT

We have recently been urged by the Ministry of Information to engage in the spread of cheerful stories, and we do not think that any more cheerful stories revealing the splendid morale of the people of this country could be told them those related by a chief-constable and a provost at a Sunday meeting of the town council in a south-east of Scotland burgh which was bombed by a Nazi raider on Saturday.

"I do not know if we are all made of the same mettle as the people of that bombed area, but if we are, then we have no fears for the morale of the people of this country," said the chief-constable. He told of how, while searching through the wrecked houses, he came upon two men groping about a bedroom in the dark. "We are strangers," they told him; "and we are looking out for our working claes for our work in the morning."

The chief-constable met a man, who was bleeding badly, carrying a bird in a cage from one of the houses. "Is the bird alive?" asked the chief-constable. "Thank God, it is," said the man, and he still held on to the cage as he was being taken away to a first-aid post.

The chief-constable told of how he found the women of the area joking and laughing together, and telling each other how they had been blown out of bed by the blast from the explosion.

After paying tribute to the courage of the families who had been rendered homeless, the provost told the council that one resident was found swearing to himself outside his wrecked house. When asked what was wrong, the man replied: "If Hitler had only told me he was coming he would have saved me a lot of bother. I just finished re-painting my house last night."

It was revealed at the meeting that the families rendered homeless had all been re-housed by 9 o'clock on Saturday evening, and that the women were almost overcome by the wonderful kindness shown to them by their fellow citizens.

Going Away to Fight, change at home.

When the war was declared on 3rd of September 1939 the people of Stirling were going about their ordinary business and little could they know how long the war was going to last. 'It will be over by Christmas' was the common belief at the time.

> I was feeding my younger son and listening to the radio when the announcement came over saying that we were therefore at war with Germany. It wasn't a surprise by any means, but my younger son was almost exactly a year old, and my heart sank. We didn't know exactly what was going to happen, it all sounded so dreadful..

In 1939 all men aged 18 to 41 could be called up for service in the armed forces. In December 1941 the upper age was raised to 51. Men working in some occupations like mining were exempted from conscription.

> When they first began to mobilise married men, they started if you had one of a family you went sooner than two, so we had three and my husband was in a reserved job as an insurance inspector.

From Stirling many men joined the Argylls seeing action in France. For those left at home waiting for news, times were very hard;

> Well, his war work was of a manner that I knew very little about it but I only had messages from time to time when he was moving ...he barely survived the war and died because of his experiences during the war.

For those men not called up many changed jobs and even more joined voluntary organisations like the Local Defence Volunteers, the Home Guard or the Air Raid Precaution unit. This woman recalls her husband's duties at Balmaha;

My husband was an air raid warden. We had patrol boats on the water and he was the liaison between headquarters and the patrol boats. We had the warning system, when the alert came over the telephone he had to go out and wind the alarm to warn people to go into their shelters.

NUMBER		SURNAME
SLV	17342781	RAE

CHRISTIAN NAMES (first only in full)
Thomas P.

CLASS CODE A

FULL POSTAL ADDRESS
52, Upper Bridge Street
Stirling

HOLDER'S SIGNATURE
Thomas P. Rae

CHANGES OF ADDRESS. No entry except by National Registration Officer, to whom removal must be notified.

REMOVED TO (Full Postal Address)

REMOVED TO (Full Postal Address)

REMOVED TO (Full Postal Address)

REMOVED TO (Full Postal Address)

REMOVED TO (Full Postal Address)

FOR OFFICIAL ENTRY ONLY (apart from Holder's Signature). ANY OTHER ENTRY OR ANY ALTERATION, MARKING OR ERASURE, IS PUNISHABLE BY A FINE OR IMPRISONMENT OR BOTH.

BUCKINGHAM PALACE

    The Queen and I offer you our heartfelt sympathy in your great sorrow.

    We pray that your country's gratitude for a life so nobly given in its service may bring you some measure of consolation.

George R.I

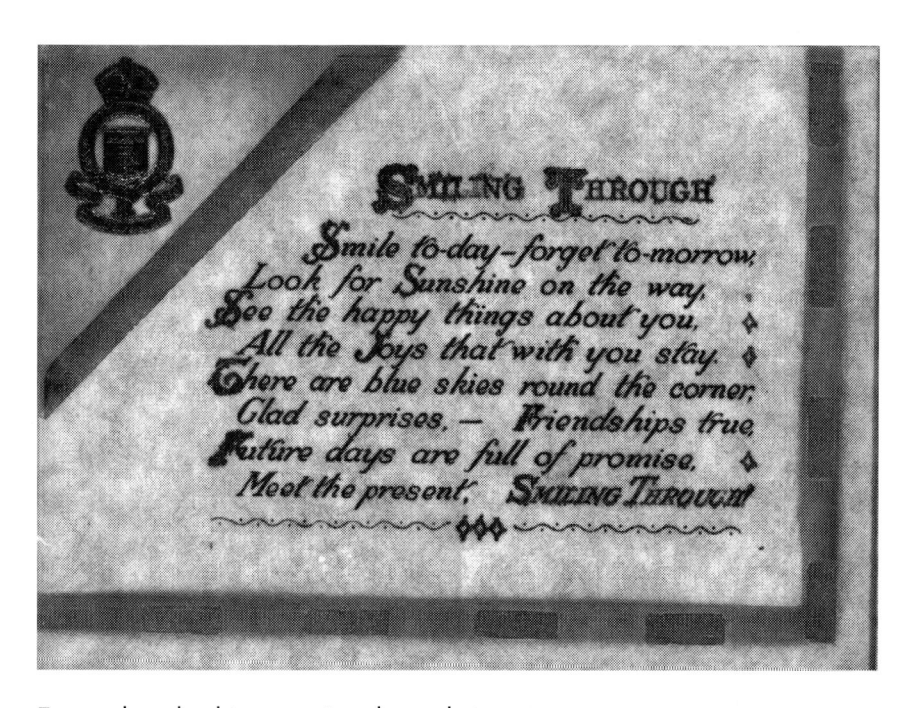

> **Smiling Through**
>
> Smile to-day – forget to-morrow,
> Look for Sunshine on the way,
> See the happy things about you,
> All the Joys that with you stay.
> There are blue skies round the corner,
> Glad surprises, – Friendships true,
> Future days are full of promise,
> Meet the present, Smiling Through!

Every close had its appointed warden;

> I was in George Street at the time, that's in the Craigs and when the war broke out I was a warden at the bottom of our stair. The warden attended all the ambulance classes. If the siren went off they all came to my house, all the people from the stair. We had to sit there until you got word, the all clear.

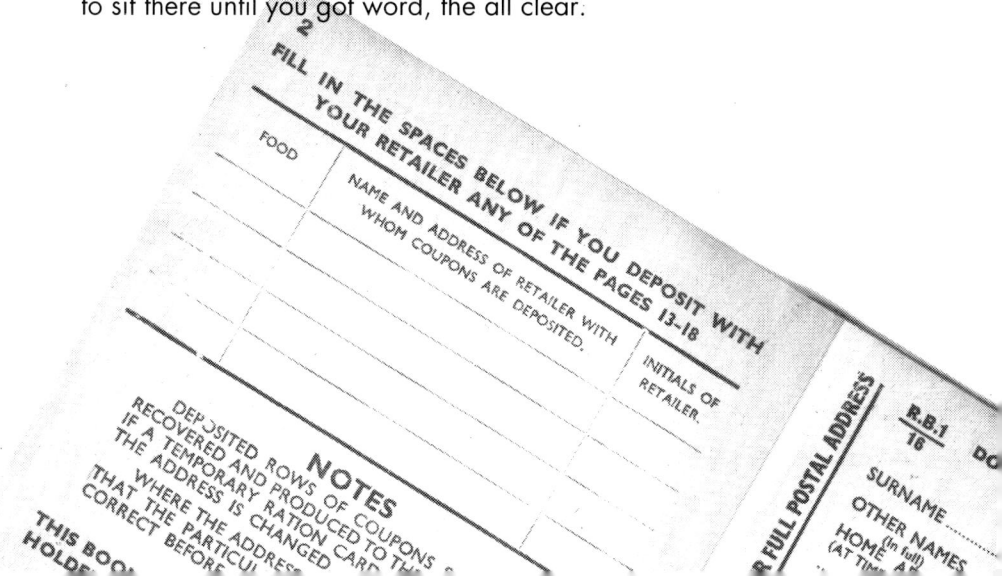

E.14.

Callander Charity Parade.

Women too were involved in this change. Some joined the armed forces like this woman :

> I thought "Ah I must go and fight I must go and do something." And there were a lot of young men saying, "I'm not going to do anything when I'm called up". I thought what a weak lot." So I went along to the recruiting office and I joined the WAAF, that was that. So, I had a gorgeous war.

On the home front they became firewatchers like this woman from Stirling

> The first night they had practice, it was in the detention barracks up beside the Holy Rude Church. And they put a bomb in the middle to see what I would do with it and shut the door. I was shut in with it and I crawled on my tummy with my tin hat on, and a pair of dungarees of my husband's, crawled in and put the bomb out within three minutes. When you're putting a fire out, never throw your water in the middle, always roundabout - it doesnae spread.

They raised money to buy arms for the men at the front. Practically every village in Stirlingshire had a Spitfire fund where money was raised by various means, coffee mornings, sales of work, concerts etc. to collect enough money for a spitfire. War weapons funds were collected in Menstrie, Kippen, Cowie, who had a warship fund, Drymen, Gartmore and countless other smaller communities as well as Stirling.

It was in the area of paid work that women's lives changed most dramatically. It was not only men that were mobilised. At the beginning of the war it was expected that women would automatically respond to the demand for their labour without direct government intervention. But this did not happen and there was a period of unemployment for women between 1939 and 1941. What happened in Stirling was that those industries which had traditionally employed women, like textile manufacture were contracted to concentrate on the war industries but women did not automatically move from their original work to war work. The first step towards compulsory mobilisation of women came in March 1941 when women aged 19-40 were invited to register with the employment exchange and would if the need arose be given a job. The upper age was raised to 50 in 1943 as labour became more difficult to hire.

This 'conscription' of women resulted in women being involved in all sorts of unusual or traditionally masculine jobs as this Dunblane lady recalls;

WOMEN NAVVIES

MOOTED AT STIRLING CONFERENCE

SCOTTISH ROAD ENGINEERS CONFER.

The view that unless the local authorities could get the Government to allow them to proceed with a limited programme of housing work, the building industry was bound to disintegrate was expressed by Mr Peter Tinto, A.R.I.B.A., research architect, Glasgow Corporation Housing Department, when he spoke on Friday on alternative methods of house construction at the annual meeting in the Golden Lion Hotel, Stirling, of the Scottish branch of the Institution of Municipal and County Engineers. Mr William Kirkland, county road surveyor, Crieff, presided at the meeting, which was attended by 150 members and representatives from Scottish local authorities. The national president of the Institution, Mr James Johnston, borough surveyor, Rawstenstall, was one of the visitors.

Dealing in his presidential address with some of the difficulties experienced by local authorities on account of shortage of personnel and the financial situation. Mr Kirkland said he noticed that one council had been considering the employment of women for certain classes of raod work. This, to his mind, was perfectly feasible. He recalled that during the last war women were employed on these jobs, even to the extent of spraying tar-macadam. Mr Kirkland said they must look ahead and ensure that post-war planning was more carefully thought out than it was at the end of the last war, so that there might be a proper absorption of demobilised soldiers when they returned to civil life.

I was actually putting shells down a chute and it was to pare off the nose of the shell and if it went in the wrong way the piston would go up in smoke. My machine was always going up in smoke, ohhh! I was literally terrified of those machines. So I was. They were huge enormous things . . .

This woman became a postwoman in Stirling during the war; As the war went on we all looked for a wee job. Like everybody else I went out; eventually I landed in the post office. Sometimes you had heavy deliveries . . . I was in Randolph Terrace and Victoria Square which was quite a busy place . . . It was a blue uniform, a blue skirt, eventually trousers but I never liked trousers. The first hats were a scream, big hats turned up at the side.

Rationing

Rationing of food was introduced in 1940 and ration books issued to the civilian population. The allowance fluctuated but a typical example was in the summer of 1941, 4oz. bacon, 8oz sugar, 2oz tea, 8oz fats, 2oz cheese and 1/- worth of meat. There were also categories of special rations for example, for expectant mothers. Children under 5 were allowed half of the adult ration. There were some ways of obtaining more than the basic allowance;

> Rationing was a terrible thing, and I don't think that anybody could safely say that they never took an extra two pound of sugar, or an extra quarter of tea in a shop. The folks said don't say anything about it, but it wasn't stealing because you were paying for it, but you werenae supposed to get it because maybe your ration would be up. Well, you got your two ounce of tea, that didn't do very much, but if you had a big family, if they all took sugar, it was hopeless. So you got your black market, sugar and tea.

HOUSEWIVES!!

**HELP TO WIN THE WAR
by
SAVING ALL WASTE**

It is now compulsary that **PAPER, BONES** and **TIN** be collected and put out according to order issued by Cleansing Department.

Place these materials outside your house every **TUESDAY** and **THURSDAY** and on these days refrain from putting out ordinary household refuse.

DO YOUR VERY BEST!

THE FOOD PROBLEM

A few weeks ago I purchased a lettuce. When I learned that the cost was one shilling, I decided that any future lettuces I ate would all be my own work. I spent fourpence on seed and in a few weeks I had a good crop, and have had lettuce daily and will continue to do so for many weeks to come. A second crop has been sown and is under way. The total cost for seed is still under the shilling I paid for that first mentioned purchase. So, if you have any ground at all, certainly dig for victory.

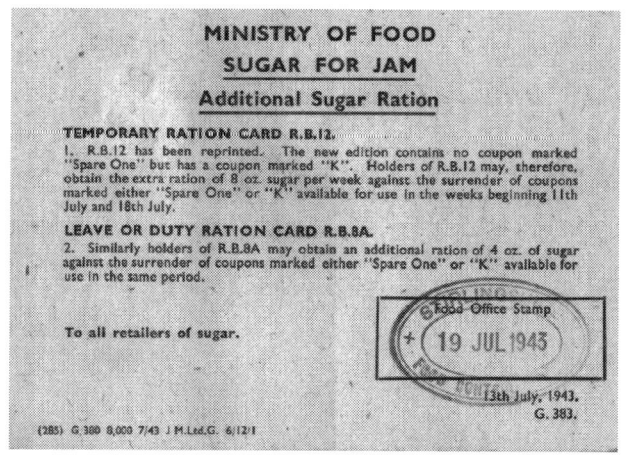

You will find hints and recipes for many simple and interesting ways to use us and other foods
... IN THE NEWS
read FOOD FACTS in the newspapers every week.
... ON THE AIR
listen to the Kitchen Front Talks at 8.15 am weekdays.

MINISTRY OF FOOD
SUGAR FOR JAM
Additional Sugar Ration

TEMPORARY RATION CARD R.B.12.
1. R.B.12 has been reprinted. The new edition contains no coupon marked "Spare One" but has a coupon marked "K". Holders of R.B.12 may, therefore, obtain the extra ration of 8 oz. sugar per week against the surrender of coupons marked either "Spare One" or "K" available for use in the weeks beginning 11th July and 18th July.

LEAVE OR DUTY RATION CARD R.B.8A.
2. Similarly holders of R.B.8A may obtain an additional ration of 4 oz. of sugar against the surrender of coupons marked either "Spare One" or "K" available for use in the same period.

To all retailers of sugar.

19 JUL 1943

13th July, 1943.
G. 383.

(285) G.380 8,000 7/43 J M.Ltd.G. 6/12/1

If the family was large rationing created extra problems;

> At that time I'd eight of a family to bring up. I'd eight books in the Co-operative and eight books with the butcher . . . it was a case of sometimes there were shops getting odd things that the Co-operative didn't get. With the result I put four books into the Buttercup in Stirling. So I'd maybe get a tin of pears, at the Co-operative all I got was sauce, or something like that, so you just went from shop to shop.

There were other ways of supplementing the rations;

> Then we got permission to keep hens, I was in Hazlebank Gardens at the time, so I kept hens so I had eggs all during the war. I had a good garden. I had all my own vegetables, and I grew strawberries with the result I could always help my mother...

People were encouraged to grow their own vegetables during the war, 'Dig for Victory' was a catchphrase of the time.

The Ministry of Food issued regular tips and recipes to housewives on how to use their rations imaginatively. The 'Kitchen Front' was on the wireless every morning at 8.15 with recipes such as Woolton Pie named after Lord Woolton, the Minister of Food.

- COFFEE -

At the present time, owing to the temporary shortage of Tea, we would recommend our Customers to economise in their purchases of Tea and buy COFFEE.

COFFEE is cheaper than Tea, and is as easily made if you follow the undernoted simple instructions:-

Take an earthenware coffee jug, rinse the jug well with hot water, the add 1 $\frac{1}{4}$ tablespoonfuls of freshly ground Coffee to every pint required or 2 tablespoonfuls for "after dinner" Coffee. Pour on boiling water, and stir while doing so; allow five minutes to stand on hot plate (not to boil), when it is ready for serving with cream or milk.

Our COFFEES are carefully selected, roasted and ground daily on our premises, and can be depended upon for Quality, Purity, and Absolute Freshness.

D. & J. MACEWEN & CO.,
STIRLING ::   And Branches.

RATIONING
of Clothing, Cloth, Footwear
from June 1, 1941

Rationing has been introduced, not to deprive you of your needs, but to make more certain that you get your share of the country's goods—to get fair share with everybody else.

When the shops re-open you will be able to buy cloth, clothes, footwear and knitting wool only if you bring your Food Ration Book with you. The shopkeeper will detach the required number of coupons from the unused margarine page. Each margarine coupon counts as one coupon towards the purchase of clothing or footwear. You will have a total of 66 coupons to last you for a year; so go sparingly. You can buy where you like and when you like without registering.

NUMBER OF COUPONS NEEDED

Men and Boys	Adult	Child	Women and Girls	Adult	Child
Unlined mackintosh or cape	9	7	Lined machintoshes or coats (over 28in. in length)	14	11
Other mackintoshes, or raincoat, or overcoat	16	11	Jacket, or short coat (under 28in. in length)	11	8
Coat, or jacket or blazer or like garment	13	8	Dress, or gown, or frock—woollen	11	8
Waistcoat, or pull-over, or cardigan, or jersey	5	3	Dress, or gown, or frock other material	7	5
Trousers (other than fustian or corduroy)	8	6	Gymtunic, or girl's skirt with bodice	8	6
Fustian or corduroy trousers	5	5	Blouse, or sports shirt, or cardigan, or jumper	5	3
Shorts	5	3	Skirt or divided skirt	7	5
Overalls, or dungarees or like garment	6	4	Overalls or dungarees or like garment	6	4
Dressing-gown or bathing gown	8	6	Apron, or pinafore	3	2
Night-shirt or pair of pyjamas	8	6	Pyjamas	8	6
Shirt, or combinations—woollen	8	6	Nightdress	6	5
Shirt, or combinations—other material	5	4	Petticoat, or slip, or combination, or cami-knickers	4	3
Pants, or vest, or bathing costume or childs blouse	4	2	Other undergarments, including corsets	3	2
Pair of socks or stockings	3	1	Pair of stockings	2	1
Collar, or tie, or pair of cuffs	1	1	Pair of socks (ankle length)	1	1
Two handkerchiefs	1	1	Collar, or tie, or pair of cuffs	1	1
Scarf, or pair of gloves or mittens	2	2	Two handkerchiefs	1	1
Pair or slippers or goloshers	4	2	Scarf, or pair of gloves or mittens or muff	2	2
Pair of boots or shoes	7	3	Pair of slippers, boots or shoes	5	3
Pair of leggings, gaiters or spats	3	2			

CLOTH Coupons needed per yard depend on the width. For example, a yard of woollen cloth 36 inches wide requires 3 coupons. The same amount of cotton or other cloth needs 2 coupons.

KNITTING WOOL. 1 coupon for 2 ounces.

THESE GOODS MAY BE BOUGHT *WITHOUT* COUPONS

*Childrens clothing of sizes generally suitable for infants less than 4 years old. *Boiler suits and workmen's bib and brace overalls. *Hats and caps. *Sewing thread. *Mending wool and mending silk. *Boot and shoe laces. *Tapes, braids, ribbons and other fabrics of 3 inches or less in width. *Elastic. *Lace and lace net. *Sanitary towels. *Braces, suspenders and garters. *Hard haberdashery. *Clogs. *Black-out cloth dyed black. *All second-hand articles.

Special Notice to Retailers

Retailers will be allowed to get fresh stocks of cloth up to and including June 18th, of other rationed goods up to and including June 21st, WITHOUT SURRENDERING COUPONS. After those dates they will be able to obtain fresh stocks only by turning in their customers' coupons. Steps have been taken, in the interests of the smaller retailers, to limit during these periods the quantity of goods which can be supplied by a wholesaler or manufacturer to any one retailer however large his orders. Further information can be obtained from your Trade Organisations.

ISSUE BY THE BOARD OF TRADE

Tea and Coffee

Cup of Tea (freshly infused) 3d
Pot of Tea for Two, Three, Four, Six or more, 4d for each person
Glass of Russian Tea 4d
Cup of Coffee (made with milk) .... Small, 3d; Large, 5d
Cup of Chocolate .... Small, 5d; Large, 7d
Glass of Milk 3d

Sweets
(IN TEN MINUTES)

Omlettes .... Savoury, 10d; Sweet, 1/-
Rum Omlette 1/9
Pancakes 9d

Savouries
(IN TEN MINUTES)

Poached Egg on Toast 8d
Scrambled Eggs on Tost .... 8d and 1/-
Welsh Rarebit 8d
Scotch Woodcock 9d
Anchovies on Toast 10d
Eggs a la Suisse .... 8d and 1/-

Fish and Cold Meat

Filleted Haddock or Plaice, with Potatoes 1/6
Ham and Egg 1/6
Cold Meat 1/3

Ices
(IN SEASON)

Plain Ice 6d
Cream Ice 9d
American Sundaes 1/-

Aerated Waters

Lemonade, Ginger Beer, Soda Water, Stone Ginger 4d
Ross's Ginger Ale 5d
Lemon Squash 8d
American Fruit Drinks, Iced 7d

Cakes

Bread and Butter .... 2d   Roll and Butter 2d
Hot Buttered Toast .... 3d   Pancakes 1d
Hot Buttered Scones . 1 $^{1}/_{2}$d   Scones 1d
Plain and Fancy Cakes (all baked in our own kitchens) 2d
Buns—Plain, Fruit, and Iced .... 1 $^{1}/_{2}$d
Butter .... 1d   Cream 2d

Wartime Menu, Golden Lion Hotel.

EGGLESS, FATLESS WALNUT CAKE

4 cups flour
1 cup chopped walnuts
1 good cup milk
1 cup sugar
4 teaspoons baking powder
1 good pinch salt

Mix flour, sugar and chopped walnuts together. Add salt and baking powder, then the milk. It should be slightly wetter than an ordinary cake mixture. Leave to rise for 10 minutes. Bake in a greased cake tin in a slow oven till risen and brown.

RECIPE of the WEEK

CARROT-CAP SALAD

Every woman who values her good complexion should have this salad regularly.

Cook two or three good sized potatoes in their skins. When tender, strain without drying off to avoid making them floury. Slice and dice neatly; then dress in vinaigrette dressing (two parts of salad oil to one of vinegar, pepper and salt to taste) while they are still hot. Pile in a salad bowl lined with a few shredded lettuce leaves of water cress. Sprinkle with a little chives or rings of spring onion and pile high with grated carrot. To make a more substantial dish, add one or two boned sardines or fillets of smoked herring.

Woolton Pie

Dice and cook about 1lb of potatoes, cauliflower and carrots. Arrange in a pie dish. Add a little vegetable extract and 1oz rolled oats to the vegetable water. Cook until thickened and pour over the vegetables. Top with mashed potato and a very little grated cheese and cook until brown.

Many ingenious recipes and ingredients were used during the war and substitutes found for almost every rationed commodity. Dried egg instead of fresh, soya flour instead of ground almonds, potatoes instead of fats in pastry, carrots in cakes instead of sugar, even parsnips instead of meat in sandwiches!

Of course food was not the only thing to be affected by rationing, clothes rationing was also introduced. Clothing was rationed from June 1941 and the utility scheme introduced in 1942 which laid down regulations on length of skirts, material to be used, fastenings to be used etc.

Some things were impossible to get, like nylon stockings;

> My mother used to tan ours [legs] for the dancing. She used to stand you up on the bunker and rub your legs with the tan and put a pencil mark down the back and then see when you came in, you had to go into the sink and stand and wash it off or she wouldnae let you get into the white sheets.

As with food, substitutes were found;

> We went to the Army & Navy stores and we bought an army blanket, my pal and I, and we made a coat and we done it all by hand, we made a coat each . . . it was like three quarters with a tie belt. But there were no buttons it was just a swing coat with a tie belt.

Rationing continued until 1954 for many products, food and clothing.

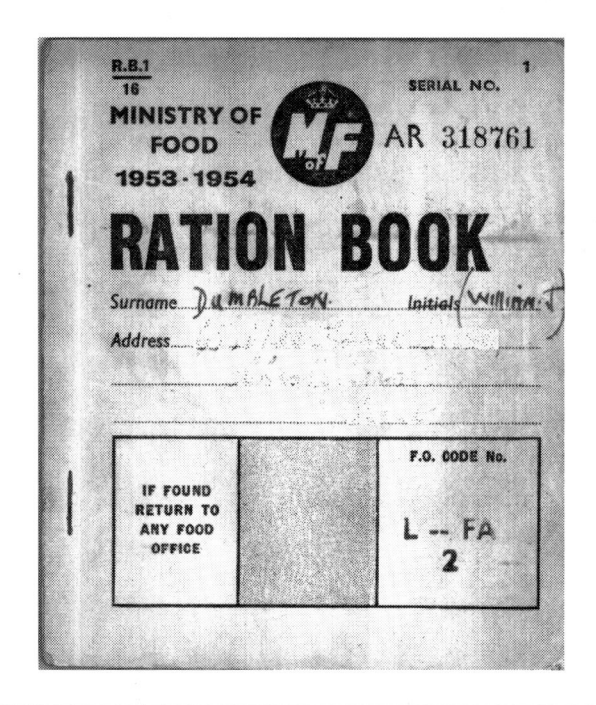

NAMES AND ADDRESSES OF RETAILERS			
AT H. POXON,	H. POXON,		
GREEN LANE	GOLDEN LANE		

EGGS

Counterfoil for **EGGS**
Initials WJ
R.B.1
16

DER'S
Name DUMBLETON

ress ...STREET...

R.B.1
16

TEA

If you deposit this page fill in overleaf

	12	11	10	9	8	7	6	5
EGGS			3				2	
	Surname and Initials							
FATS	12	11	10					2
			3					
	Surname and Initials							
	12	11	10	9	8			2

---

22 IF FOUND RETURN TO ANY FOOD OFFICE

Do not cut out coupons
THE SHOPKEEPER WILL DO THIS FOR YOU

D6	D6	D6	D6	E6	E6	E6	E6
D5	D5	D5	D5	E5	E5	E5	E5
D4	D4	D4	D4	E4	E4	E4	E4
D3	D3	D3	D3	E3	E3	E3	E3
D2	D2	D2	D2	E2	E2	E2	E2
D1	D1	D1	D1	E1	E1	E1	E1

R.B.11
16

PERSO

Food Office Co

Surname and Initials......
This page may be detache
you should fill in details abo

E13	E13	E1
E12	E12	E1
E11	E11	E
E10	E10	E1
E9	E9	E9
E8	E8	E8
E7	E7	E7

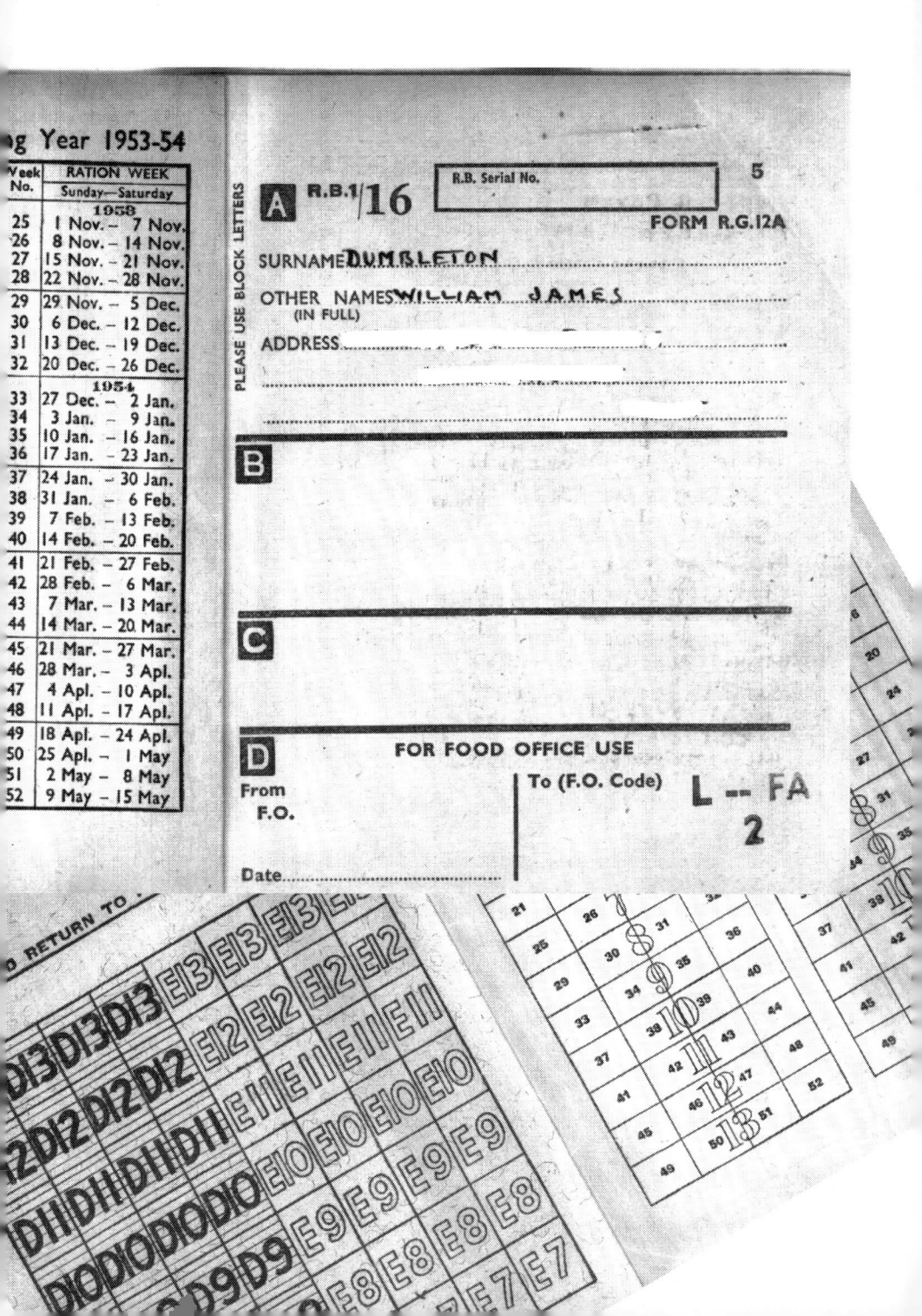

Week No.	RATION WEEK Sunday—Saturday
	1953
25	1 Nov. – 7 Nov.
26	8 Nov. – 14 Nov.
27	15 Nov. – 21 Nov.
28	22 Nov. – 28 Nov.
29	29 Nov. – 5 Dec.
30	6 Dec. – 12 Dec.
31	13 Dec. – 19 Dec.
32	20 Dec. – 26 Dec.
	1954
33	27 Dec. – 2 Jan.
34	3 Jan. – 9 Jan.
35	10 Jan. – 16 Jan.
36	17 Jan. – 23 Jan.
37	24 Jan. – 30 Jan.
38	31 Jan. – 6 Feb.
39	7 Feb. – 13 Feb.
40	14 Feb. – 20 Feb.
41	21 Feb. – 27 Feb.
42	28 Feb. – 6 Mar.
43	7 Mar. – 13 Mar.
44	14 Mar. – 20 Mar.
45	21 Mar. – 27 Mar.
46	28 Mar. – 3 Apl.
47	4 Apl. – 10 Apl.
48	11 Apl. – 17 Apl.
49	18 Apl. – 24 Apl.
50	25 Apl. – 1 May
51	2 May – 8 May
52	9 May – 15 May

Year 1953-54

A R.B.1/16   R.B. Serial No.   5

FORM R.G.12A

PLEASE USE BLOCK LETTERS

SURNAME **DUMBLETON**

OTHER NAMES **WILLIAM JAMES**
(IN FULL)

ADDRESS ....

B

C

D   FOR FOOD OFFICE USE

From F.O.   To (F.O. Code)   L – FA   2

Date..........................

Evacuees

Not many children were evacuated from Stirling although after the bomb hit the King's Park football ground some children were sent away;

> We sent him away because there were two bombs dropped on Stirling and we thought, "Well at least one will be safe, if anything happens". He was about thirteen at the time, and he was there 'til he was fourteen.

Stirling did get quite a number of evacuees from Glasgow. These children came mainly from the East End from poor families and caused quite a stir;

> The children were evacuated from Glasgow to our school, the Whins of Milton. Its not right to say this about Glasgow but they were rough and ready. You can imagine what it was like and we were terrified what was going to happen to our own kids . . . we were frightened that they would get germs and things . . . you would go and comb their hair, the kid's hair every night . . .

Some evacuees came from more exotic locations;

> I had one evacuee sent to me she was about fifteen, she was a German. Hannah was her name and I used to wonder sometimes she seemed to get letters from all over the world . . . Well, Hannah went to the High School, I think she was a German first and a Jewess second despite what had been done to her people because she used to listen to the German news and I'd see her looking elated if one of our destroyers had been sunk and I'd say "Who's side are you on?" She said " Well of course you're first of all a German". . . . However, eventually, Stirling was becoming a protected area so any aliens were to be taken out of Stirling and the police came one day while she was at school and they had a warrant to search her room and they turned everything upside down and she was only allowed to stay for half a day after that . . . I never heard anymore about her . . .

During the war all Germans, Jewish and gentile were under suspicion and many of them were interred for the duration of the war.

8th June, 1946

To-day, as we celebrate victory, I send this personal message to you and all other boys and girls at school. For you have shared in the hardships and dangers of a total war and you have shared no less in the triumph of the Allied Nations.

I know you will always feel proud to belong to a country which was capable of such supreme effort; proud, too, of parents and elder brothers and sisters who by their courage, endurance and enterprise brought victory. May these qualities be yours as you grow up and join in the common effort to establish among the nations of the world unity and peace.

George R.I.

The End of the War

After six years of war, in May 1945, Germany surrendered although Japan didn't surrender until August that year. For those at home times had been hard. There was great relief that the years of blackout, gasmasks, rationing and air raid shelters were finally over. Stirling people celebrated in style, King Street was a mass of bunting and street parties were held throughout the district, this lady remembers Cowie on V.E. day;

> When we had peace we had a bonfire. We'd collected wood for about a fortnight, my father lit the fire because he was the oldest resident . . . and we danced . . . dancing singing songs. Oh, we had a great night and they were dancing eightsome reels in the streets and of course all the men got going with their bottles of beer . . .